BRUISED, MISUSED & RENEWED
A HEALED WOMAN'S STORY

GLORIA D. SIMMONS

Bruised, Misused & Renewed
Copyright © 2024 by Gloria D. Simmons

All rights reserved. No part of this book may be reproduced or transmitted in any form or by any means without written permission from the author.

ISBN 979-8-9866703-8-6

Printed in USA
Published by SIP Publications, LLC and Junior Authors
Designed by 5.13 Graphics & Media, LLC
https://www.thejuniorauthors.com/sip-publications-llc.htm

Dedication

I dedicate this book to God, the father of us all; my deceased parents, Thurman and Clara Simmons; my daughters, Tjuana Simmons and JaQuan Postell; my grandchildren, Victoria Evans and Rhema Postell; my siblings, Doretha, Crystal, William, Melitsa, Thurman, Vernon, and Veronica. I also dedicate this book to all the people who supported me through the detrimental events that have shaped my life and are mentioned in this book: Gwennette Johnson, Diane Williams, Daphne A. Morgan, Connie Miller, Roger Asterino, and Pastor Calvin A. Harper.

To everyone I may not have directly mentioned who has supported me, I love you all dearly. I pray this book brings God's healing, hope, and restoration to everyone who reads it.

Contents

Foreword..i

Introduction...iii

Chapter 1 – Bruised......................................1

Chapter 2 – Life Between Marriages......................13

Chapter 3 – My Baby's Daddy.............................22

Chapter 4 – My Second Marriage..........................27

Chapter 5 – Single Life.................................38

Chapter 6 – Life Goes On................................45

Chapter 7 – Led by God..................................51

Chapter 8 – Relationships...............................56

FOREWORD BY HAROLD L. JONES

Behind every dark cloud comes a silver lining. I've known author Gloria Simmons for decades and never saw the pain hidden behind her glorious personality as she always presented herself as the self-assured, assertive, and ideal mother and friend. She was always there in any time of need.

Bruised, Misused and Renewed not only addresses so many myths that have haunted African American families for centuries, but it also brilliantly serves to demystify the erroneous thoughts regarding suicide, abortion, and other thoughts that have caused pain throughout many Black households. Many Black families have lost loved ones to suicide, and never allowing men to seek psychological or spiritual direction needed to address these issues only heightens the problem. This book addresses the complications of Black life and provides statistical data to back up these claims.

So often, I resent the characterization of Black women being identified as "STRONG BLACK WOMEN." Often, these titles are given to Black women who have raised their children as single parents. But Simmons at no time has portrayed herself as "Super Woman," nor has she bashed men, nor has she negatively attached labels to Black men because of her abusive past. This is a story about a young, determined widow who turned a life plagued by suffering into a temple for women everywhere who are searching to survive.

Bruised, Misused and Renewed is a must-read for everyone searching to identify who they are. This book provides hope for all, especially young women who see no way out of the many dilemmas that confront them. Gloria Simmons is living testimony to all women and men that we can make this planet a better place if we just put in the effort!

Introduction

I was very apprehensive about writing this book with all the details about myself, but I was encouraged by both my daughters, who felt like I never healed from childhood tragedies. I'm encouraged to help others who may need to heal. I realize that many times, we go through trials that God knows we'll get through for the benefit of others. I thought I was healed; I thought the effects of all the pain had healed over time. However, even though much time has passed, putting the hurt, pain, and mental anguish in writing has brought back vivid memories. It's as if it all just happened yesterday.

This journey has brought me closer to God. I now realize how painful and prolonged suffering after the death of a loved one can last. I know God loves us and that He won't put more on any of us than He knows we can bear. Pastor C. A. Harper would say, "Before we receive it, God tests it, tries it, then gives it to us." God allowing me to survive certainly proved that He tried and tested the trials and tribulations before I had to endure them. Now, I'm here to share my testimony. If my children or grandchildren take that to heart, they'll endure life knowing how great God is and how much He cares and protects us.

My youngest daughter would share my story when educating high school students about relationships. One day, she asked what had happened and why I had never married again after divorcing her dad. I told her I was a widow and divorcee at the age of twenty-six. I refused to bring a man into our lives unless I was sure he was a God-fearing man and that I could trust him with my children. He needed to be someone who really loved me and my children. She responded by telling me that my children were women now and that I deserved to live my life.

When I asked her what she tells her students she said, "There was a girl who was raised in a very spiritual home with seven siblings and loving parents. This girl married her high school sweetheart, who was a football player and co-captain of the football team. They married right after they graduated from high school. Everyone thought it was a marriage made in heaven until her high school sweetheart committed suicide, leaving her alone and trying to explain his death to all their friends and family. After him, she remarried a man who was abusive and divorced him within three years." She said she concludes the story with, "That girl is my mother!" After hearing her tell my story, I decided that it was time to tell her my story in its entirety.

Today, my daughter has a book publishing company. After writing and publishing several books of her own, numerous adults also requested that she publish their books. I think that's why she has continuously asked me to write this book. With her encouragement, I began to reflect upon my story, hoping that this would help me and others heal. There's nothing more fear-inducing in telling my story than what I already experienced regarding what people said and will say about me. However, I know that this will be healing for me. Re-experiencing the traumatic agony is horrific; I recognize the pain once again felt fifty years ago, but writing has been a key part of my healing process.

The majority of my friends, family, and acquaintances probably think I was already healed, but in reality, I was not. I can hide it well; I can be the light of a party, and I crack funny jokes. I've been told I'm brutally honest and say it like it is, even if it's hurtful. Most of my friends say I'm smart, intelligent, enthusiastic, and that I know my stuff. My closest friends would add that I'm a little crazy. I thank God for my sense of humor and the honesty that experience has afforded me.

BRUISED, MISUSED & RENEWED

A HEALED WOMAN'S STORY

Chapter 1

BRUISED

BOOM!

"John, are you ok?" I asked. There was no answer, so I ran from the kitchen to our bedroom. There, I found my husband at the foot of our bed, blood pouring out of his head. I put my face to his face and tried to stop the blood while I screamed for help. My upstairs neighbor heard me and began banging on our door. I opened the door covered in blood and asked, "Can you help him?"

He ran in and said, "I'll call an ambulance." That was the last night I would see my nineteen-year-old husband alive.

The year was 1969, and I was attending Woodward High School on a special transfer. This was the year I met my high school sweetheart. He was from the right side of the district, and we first saw each other in the school hallway. Shortly thereafter, he asked for my phone number. From that day on, we were together until his death on January 22, 1973.

We were like peas and carrots, like white on rice, like steak and potatoes—meant to be together. He was the reason I had the best attendance record my entire time in high school. I knew being absent from school meant a day without seeing my man, and I was not going to do that. I could've graduated the year before I did, but again, I didn't want to go a day without seeing him. Every day, we met in between classes and had lunch together. He had a little Ford Falcon, and he'd drive home each day, or we would hang out after school at his house or mine.

Having a high school sweetheart was cool, and it also boosted my self-esteem. I had a boyfriend before meeting John, but he didn't go to my high school. All my high school friends knew John, and that made me feel special—especially since he was the co-captain of the football team that had won the league for the last six years.

Life was great; I was privileged and had everything going for me. John and I dated for the last two or so years of high school. Throughout those years, he drove to and from school in his Falcon Ford, and I was always the co-passenger. He eventually taught me how to drive a stick shift. As our relationship developed, we would have dinner together at his parent's home or mine. Once we left each other for the evening, we'd talk on the phone until we fell asleep, and then we'd do it all again the next day.

We were so in love, and we never got bored with each other. Sometimes, we would go to a local park and play on the swings. Other times, we just sat in the car and talked about our life together and what we would do when we got married. Anyway, we really thought we were in love. In our minds, there was no one to live for but each other.

We continued our daily routine until graduation. Once we graduated, we got very serious and became engaged. We were very much in love (or at least we thought so). Our wedding was held on September 23, 1972. It was small and quaint—just enough for us but not for his parents. Our so-called reception was held at his parents' house. It was nothing special, and anyway, we were too anxious to get back to our apartment to care.

By then, we both had jobs and a new routine. We rode to and from work together, and then we'd stop by my parents' home before going to our apartment. Every day, I'd cook dinner, clean up, take a shower, and get ready for work the next day. On weekends, we partied like there was no tomorrow. On Sundays, we went to his church, then my church, and then we ate and relaxed and started all over the next week.

Our routine was never boring to us, but it didn't last. Our marriage only lasted four months before John committed suicide. We were still children but thought we were truly adults. We did everything and spent almost every day together. I got a job as a bookkeeper, and he began to work for his uncle's construction company. My brother-in-law had several cabs available at night, and some evenings, John would make extra cash driving people around.

One day, before we got married, we were sitting in his car in front of my parents' house. I was playing with him and told him I didn't want to get married and that we were moving too fast. He asked me why I was leading him on, pretending that I wanted to get married. I said, "I thought you would mess up, and I would get out of it." We always played little psyche games on each other, but this time, I took it too far! He started the car and raced down the dead-end street. I managed to wrestle his hands off the steering wheel, and since it was a stick shift, the car shut off before we got down to the end of the street and over the guardrail.

I looked at him, scared and out of breath. "WHAT THE HELL ARE YOU ARE DOING? YOU TRYING TO KILL US!" I screamed.

He broke down crying and said, "Don't mess with me like this!"

"We always play psyche games. What is wrong with you?"

"DON'T play with me like that again; don't play with me like this. Do you hear me? Are you going to marry me or not?"

"I was just playing; yes, we're going to get married!" I said, even though I couldn't believe his reaction. The weirdest feeling came over me, and I thought he could've killed both of us, but I married him anyway and never played with him like that ever again. This really was what they call a "red flag."

My dad didn't like the idea of us getting married right after high school. He really wanted me to go to college, but Momma was just glad I graduated from high school since neither of my older siblings did. She didn't seem to care one way or another about college. It was my decision. After all, she married my daddy when she was only seventeen. He seemed to be from a good family and had a good job working for his uncle's construction firm. My dad worked in construction all his life; it was an honest trade.

Once, I heard a minister say, "Satan wants us to be in pain, isolated, and bound in our wounds." God wants us to be free, and He gives us discernment to be free, at peace, and to love one another. You can't do any of these things if you're bound in your own wounds. That's the reason God allows things to happen; it's so that we can help each other. I saw and felt the pain of the Christian community and secular community as well. I was bound in my wounds for years after John's death. He committed suicide one day before our fourth month of marriage. That was the night I became a woman. I went from an adolescent to an adult; it was an abrupt conclusion to my childhood. Life became a living nightmare. I was forced to live very cautiously.

Now, years later, at seventy years of age, my daughter asked me to write about my story. One can't fathom the horror of writing about an experience or one's history without connecting with the past. I've gone to bed in tears. People said Black folk don't commit suicide. I'm here to tell you they did then, and they do now!

In my opinion, suicide is a very selfish, inconsiderate, egomaniacal act. Yet, at that time, I didn't think it would become so self-absorbing for me. I spent many days, weeks, months, and years trying to envision how a person could commit suicide and leave their loved ones to suffer the consequences. I never thought that people felt they had to conjure up a reason for suicidal individuals.

I avoided classmates, high school reunions, friends from high school, and anyone else who knew John. Instead, I devoted myself to work until I was so worn out that I'd go home. I'd have a few drinks, and then I was so tired that all I could do was go to bed.

Many people said cruel things about me and the suicidal act that John committed. When we were arranging his funeral, his sister said that my mom and I were voodoo bitches, and they were going to get a private detective to find out what happened. Others said we played Russian roulette, and he shot himself when playing the game. Some people even speculated that we got high and that I told him to kill himself. I felt that the world around me was so cruel that I should end my life. However, I was too naïve to know how. I felt guilty, disturbed, ignorant, and without any aspiration to go on.

Even now, fifty years later, at my first and only high school reunion, a classmate asked me why John committed suicide. "If you make it to heaven, ask him," I responded. God has kept me here for some reason, and I will continue to fight on.

In trying to understand John's suicide, I began pouring myself into research. I looked at the comparison of Black people committing suicide in comparison to white people. While I couldn't find anything in the 70s, according to the Centers of Disease Control, the unadjusted suicide rate for this period rose from a low of 11.6 suicides per 100,000 people in 1970 to a high of 13.1 in 1977. The number then declined to 11.9 in 1980. Males had a higher risk of suicide than females, and the differential between rates for males and females continued to widen.

The age-adjusted suicide rate for whites (12.1) was almost twice that for Blacks and other races (6.7). White males consistently had the highest suicide rates, with Black and other males the second highest, followed by white females and Black and other females. In 1980, 70% of suicides were among white males; 22% among white females; 6% among Black and other males; and 2% among Black and other females.[1]

In the most recent decade, the suicide rate among young Blacks has risen to the point where it is nearly as high as that of their white peers. The data in this analysis reflects the striking contrast in age distribution in the suicide patterns of whites and Blacks. Whereas white suicide increases in direct relation with advancing chronological age, suicide among Blacks reaches its peak during their younger years. Current statistics fail to reflect a "dramatic" or significant increase in the suicide rate of Black women. Contrary to popular belief, Black men in their twenties represent the most suicide-prone group. Young Black males have been committing suicide at a steadily increasing rate in the past six years. Regionally, Black suicide rates are highest in the North and West and lowest in the South. White suicide rates reflect a slightly different

---

[1] "Perspectives in Disease Prevention and Health Promotion Suicide -- United States, 1970-1980." Centers for Disease Control and Prevention, June 21, 1985. https://www.cdc.gov/mmwr/preview/mmwrhtml/00000561.htm.

regional distribution. The highest rates occur in the West and the lowest in the North.[2]

---

[2] Davis, Robert. "Black Suicide in the Seventies: Current Trends." *Suicide and Life-Threatening Behavior* 9, no. 3 (September 1979): 131–40. https://doi.org/10.1111/j.1943-278x.1979.tb00557.x.

In Memoriam

JOHN ERICK FROST

January 19, 1954   -   January 22, 1973

SERVICES:

Friday - January 26, 1973 - - - - - 2:00 P. M.

Mt. Carmel Baptist Church
3101 Eastern Avenue
Cincinnati, Ohio

Rev. T. L. Barron ----------------- Pastor

Rev. Howard Gamble ----------- Presiding

INTERMENT - Spring Grove Cemetery
Cincinnati, Ohio

OBITUARY

"The call was sudden,
The shock severe,
Little one knew such grief was near,
Only those who have lost can tell,
The pain of parting without farewell."

John Erick Frost was born in Cincinnati, Ohio, January 19, 1954 and departed this life suddenly January 22, 1973, at the age of 19 years and 3 days. He was the son of Mr. and Mrs. Eddie Lee Frost. As a youngster he attended Second Baptist Church regularly.

On September 23, 1972, he was married to Miss Gloria Simmons.

He leaves to mourn his passing, his devoted wife Mrs. Gloria Frost, his parents, Mr. and Mrs. Eddie Lee Frost, 2 sisters, Mrs. Christine Carter and Miss Julia Frost, 2 brothers, Neal and Edward Frost, his grandparents, Mr. and Mrs. Lile Bouldin, his Mother and Father-in-law, Mr. and Mrs. Thurman Simmons, 4 sisters-in-law, 3 brothers-in-law and a host of cousins, other relatives and friends.

"I turn to the almighty God,
In this my time of grief,
I do not beg for comfort,
I do not seek relief,
I only ask for courage, and the strength to bear my sorrow,
That I might still fulfill my place,
And carry on tomorrow.

I do not wish to drop my cross,
Or fall beside the way,
Just give me strength to serve thy God for still another day,
enable me to do thy will,
However great my loss,
And as thy Humble Servant of God,
To bear whatever cross.
                                    The Family

ORDER OF SERVICE

Rev. Howard Gamble - - - Presiding

Processional ....

Selection .... Choir

Prayer ....

Scripture Reading..................

Selection ....Choir

Remarks .... Rev. T. L. Barron

Solo .... Miss Melista Simmons
            Played for by Mrs. Claresa Barnes

Remarks........... Rev. George Carlton

Solo .... Mr. Wilber Woolfork

Obituary........... Mrs. Fannie Graham

Eulogy .... Rev. Howard Gamble

Recessional......................

Chapter 2

LIFE BETWEEN MARRIAGES

(Regret, Shame, Guilt, and Joy)

Months after John's death, I ran into a friend who asked me how I was doing. He wanted to know if he could stop by sometime. He knew my family, and I thought it was okay, so I said sure. Well, he stopped by one day and asked if I wanted to go to the movies. I went, and one date led to another, and eventually, I looked forward to hanging out with him. We'd talk on the phone, go out to eat, and even go bowling. It was nice to have a friend who would allow me to rattle on and on without judging me or questioning me about John's death.

One day, my mother said to me, "I hope you all are just friends."

"What else could we be?" I answered. He was much older than I was. He taught me how to bowl and keep score. I never thought of him as a boyfriend.

However, one day, while we were sitting in his car, he said, "Let's talk. You know, everybody's okay with us going out, and I think we should get more serious."

"I have to think about it and talk it over with my mother," I said.

He lied, of course, and said, "It's okay with her; she said you're doing much better accepting John's death." I didn't question her or him. We started seeing each other on a regular basis.

We really must be careful what we ask God for when we pray. I prayed that I was pregnant when John died, but I wasn't. I never thought of being pregnant by anyone but him. I sure didn't want a baby by this new man. I couldn't believe it! He was the first guy I had sexual contact with, and I got pregnant. He was so happy when I told him. Like I said before, he was much older and had a daughter whom he always questioned if she was truly his. He knew I was naïve and hurting; he took advantage of that.

He said, real solemnly, "At least I would know that it was truly my child." I started hating him that very minute. I refused to go out with him ever again. After a few weeks, Momma asked me what was wrong and why I was no longer seeing him. I told her that he was not for me. I told her that he wanted to be my boyfriend and that I knew she would not like that. She was pleased to hear that I was no longer hanging around him. I couldn't tell her I was pregnant; I knew that would hurt her. For the first time, I realized my mother was just as naïve as I was. Bless her heart.

One day, he came by the house to talk to my mother about our relationship. He got a tongue lashing from her, and she told him he couldn't ever come back! She wouldn't and didn't let him say anything to her. All she said was for him to get the hell away from us, and if she saw him around our house again, she'd call the police.

The worst part of it was I had to abort the child before she or anyone knew. I talked about getting rid of the child inside of me every day thereafter. I spoke to my close friend and even a sibling who knew a lady who knew someone who performed illegal abortions, and that was what I did. Sin so easily besets us, and it is always prevalent for its victims. I was a victim. It was even more horrific than John's death. I was sick for days; I hated what I had done. I thought I was going to die. I thought this was God's punishment.

But God's mercy and grace kept me even though I thought I had committed one of the worst sins. I was truly a murderer, and the gossip spread through my mind that I was truly capable of killing someone. Maybe I even deserved the mean-spirited gossip people had spread when John committed suicide. After I was well, I had no regrets about not having that child. That was until I became pregnant by the next guy I dated.

Between 1850 and 1880, abortions were legal for those who could afford them. Abortions did not become an issue for this country until 1880. By 1973, with Roe v. Wade, abortions became a fundamental legal right. Of course, it was not the abortion laws that I was concerned about—it was the hatred and ferocity of people in the gossip community that I thought I could not withstand. Eventually, abortions in the U.S. became an issue because they were prohibiting population growth among white Americans. Isn't it a shame that God's law was not the concern for abortions? Worried about losing their hold on the country, white men in power supported abortion bans to get upper-class white women to have more children.[3]

Anyway, I knew God would not have mercy on me this time. Talk about one episode after another! I was sin-sick! Every time I tried to live what I thought to be a normal life, one thing happened after another! The worst part of it all was that all I could think about was what people would say about me if they knew I was pregnant

---

[3] "Historical Abortion Law Timeline: 1850 to Today." Planned Parenthood Action Fund. Accessed April 9, 2024.
https://www.plannedparenthoodaction.org/issues/abortion/abortion-central-history-reproductive-health-care-america/historical-abortion-law-timeline-1850-today.

or even dating. After all, I was only twenty years old, and John died when I was eighteen.

What a mess! What on earth was a girl to do? I was a church-going child that had one thing happen after another. Yes, fornication is a sin, but I didn't think I was doing anything different than any other young lady. I felt so unrighteous and unholy in life, and the evil of this world continued to consume me. Should I not date anymore? Was I supposed to be single? Was I not to live a normal life? Was I to get rid of another child? God forbid!

I thought my mom would have a heart attack if she found out that I was pregnant. Everyone would think I was promiscuous. Again, the only thing I thought about was all the cruel gossip people had to say about me after John's death. So, I didn't tell her that I was pregnant! I thought she'd be so upset and disgusted with me. Heck, I was disgusted with myself and thought, what's the use in trying to live?

It was one night at church that God showed Momma what was happening. She said to me, "The Lord is showing me that you are thinking about taking some pills," and then she hesitated, "and I know what God's saying…" Then, she stopped mid-sentence and said, "Okay, Lord."

When we got home, she asked me, "What are you thinking about doing?" she asked. "God showed me you're having a little baby, and you better not think about taking anything to abort the child."

My boyfriend then decided to ask her if I had not told her I was pregnant. I wanted to slap the mess out of him. I knew him from school, and he knew John, which didn't make me feel any better about dating him, but he was a good friend, and I always knew he liked me. He was also on the high school football team. His locker was next to mine, and we always played and laughed around with each other at our lockers.

The first time I saw him after my John's death, I was at a department store. He immediately grabbed and hugged me without thinking about it. I thought he must not have heard what people said about me. He was so concerned about my mental health and wellness. He asked me how I had been doing and if he could have my phone number. I could see he was sincere, so I gave him my number. He called me that night and every day after. We started dating and had good times together. So much so that I felt like I was betraying my deceased husband. However, he made me feel like John would be pleased, so I continued to date him. He was patient and nice to me. He understood my feelings and was always concerned about me. I was twenty years old, and he was twenty-one. We dated as if we were high school sweethearts.

On the night we decided to finally have sex, we went to the Drake Hotel. That's where I got pregnant. I remember feeling promiscuous. I had one dramatic episode happen after another. I thought, what's a girl to do? Well, we decided to move in together because I was not going to be with anybody else.

He had gone with me to every doctor's appointment. The nurses thought he was terrific! Finally, the day came when it was time to deliver our baby. When I was in labor, he was right there with me. He stayed from 7:00 a.m. to 3:00 p.m. until I finally told him to go to work. He had told everybody at work that I was pregnant. He went to work and was supposed to get off at 11:00 p.m.

I had a hard labor and wasn't sure if I was going to make it. Death seemed to plague me every time something good happened to me. I started off having an epidural, but by the time my daughter was born, there was only one person who administered the epidural, and she was well past the end of her shift. They removed the epidural, which made the labor even harder. Finally, I was fully dilated, and they began to administer a spinal tap, but they had difficulties. They poked me about seven times in my back when, finally, a doctor came in and said, "This girl is suffering; let me give her the epidural." I remember the numbness feeling so good, and I thanked him and said that I couldn't feel the pain anymore.

Then, they told me to push and push and push! I did until someone said, "STOP! THE BABY NEEDS TO BE TURNED!" I couldn't believe it.

The doctor said, "Let me turn the baby around." He reached into me, pushed the baby back in, and turned her around!

I felt every bit of that and began to scream, "I can feel that! Lord, help me, please!"

Suddenly, I heard someone crying! It was my baby. I delivered her at 7:56 p.m. Both my parents were there. My dad started pressing on my stomach and told me that he thought there was another baby in there. There definitely wasn't. I was 98 pounds when I got pregnant and 126 after my baby's birth!

My baby's dad also ended up making it. I said, "You off work."

He said, "Yes, my boss told me to leave and get to the hospital. This is where a father should be when his baby is being born!"

During the agony of childbirth, you almost wish you were dead, and then suddenly, you forget about the pain and thank God for a healthy child! Giving birth is really a miracle. Although many young ladies think it's something that all women do, it's not. Giving birth to a child is one of the most miraculous things that can happen in one's life.

There are so many things that can go wrong, including a breech baby, miscarriage, stillbirth, ectopic pregnancy, and numerous diseases that can cause problems throughout a child's life after birth. It's funny that I still thought about all the gossip and insensitive things people could say. Do you remember that old saying: *Sticks and stones may break my bones, but words will never hurt me*? Well, that's a lie! Words not only hurt, but they can also injure you for life.

Chapter 3

MY BABY'S DADDY

I had to be an adult and face reality. I had a wonderful baby girl and someone to care for who depended on me. One day after I had Tjuana, I got home from taking her to her first checkup, and I could hardly stand up. I was weak and so cold that I stood on the heat register, holding my baby. Momma came in to find out what the doctor had said about the baby, but then she saw me, and she said, "You're sick." I had a fever and was shaking with cold chills, so Momma helped me to bed. I had the flu.

For three days, I couldn't take care of my baby or get out of bed. I thought I was dying or being punished for my sins. Thank God, between her daddy and my momma, the baby was fine. I thought, finally, I have a life filled with joy, and here comes another sickness or more trauma. Again, I thought, maybe I'm not meant to live a normal life. Every time a new beginning started, something seemed to happen to make me feel afraid to live. I told Momma how I felt like I should give up on living. Momma told me to pray every time I felt like that. She said to ask God to heal my mind and help me learn to accept life as it comes. She said I was a kid who had gone through things that older people had not experienced and that God kept me here as a testimony to others. She was always praying for me, and she cried out to God for me many times.

Sometimes, I'd hear her praying for all her children and telling God about all our issues. She never gave up on any of us. I thought she knew God personally. I learned to pray like she prayed, always starting out my prayers with, "Almighty and most Wise God, I come to you praying for my family…" I can hear her now, praying and crying for us even today. And as my baby grew, she learned to pray— it seems like— better than I ever could.

One night, about three weeks after birth, I started throwing up and felt so sick in my stomach. Momma told me, "Your eyes look dark." She made me some hot tea, put a bed pan under the toilet seat with turpentine and hot water, and told me to drink the tea and sit on the toilet. Shortly thereafter, I felt like I was having another child.

I screamed, "Momma!" She came into the bathroom and saw something hanging out of me, and you'll never guess what it was. Momma was right; packing had been left in my body, and finally, it was coming out now. Momma said push, and as I did, a lump of gauze fell out. Momma was there to save my life. Thank God for mothers—they seem to know what to do for everything. My eyes cleared up within a day, and I felt like a new person.

I began to search for jobs and got one at a bank within a few weeks. My baby's dad was there to help with her, and he had a decent job, too. He worked at night, while I worked the first shift possible at my job. In between our shifts, Momma cared for Tjuana. I couldn't wait to get home to my baby. Lots of times, when I got home, my baby and Momma were curled up together in a chair asleep. I thought Tjuana was bonding with Momma and not me, and I became jealous. Momma was doing what I could have been doing if I had been home with her, but I was still so appreciative that she was able to take care of Tjuana. I worked, came home, took care of my baby, and prayed every night for God's protection and help.

Her daddy and I got along well for two years, but our relationship changed when this lady at his job got him involved with her club. He started talking to her every night when he got home. One day, I asked him what kind of club they were part of. Why did they have to talk about it every night? He said they were planning their first event, and I'd see what it was all about soon. Well, they were planning this big fashion show. He was very fashion-conscious and dressed well. I thought it was a good business venture until the day of the show.

When I finally met the lady, I knew they weren't just planning events. I could tell they were having an affair. The fashion show was very good, and I had a really nice time. However, shortly after that night, they got into an argument regarding the money they still had to pay for the event. One thing led to another, and finally, I found out that she kept asking him for money to pay for the event—money he had to pay because they were both indebted to the venue.

One night, she called and asked to speak to me. She told me that my baby's daddy and her were lovers; they had been lovers for some time. He became mad as hell when I approached him about this. He asked her why she was telling me all these lies. He told her she was a liar and that she knew she was telling a damn lie. He even spoke with her husband that night and told him she was telling me lies about them. He said, "I have never had anything sexual with your wife, and I don't understand why she's telling my lady this shit."

Things were never the same after that night. We soon went our separate ways. He continued to be a decent dad, but our relationship was over. My momma and I talked about it one day, and she said she believed he was telling the truth because he wouldn't have spoken to her husband otherwise. We continued to be friends without being romantically involved. It's funny how distrust separates people. Once you lose trust in an individual, it's hard to get it back. It takes true love to get trust back in a relationship, and we didn't have that. I loved my baby, and that was enough love for me.

I was so glad we didn't get married. He began dating other people, and eventually, so did I, but we remained friends. I was enjoying my baby, and that was all I thought I needed. Our daughter ended up graduating as the valedictorian of her high school class. Then, she graduated from college, got married, and then we had our first grandchild. Our daughter is so loving and God-fearing. I'm so blessed to have her. Life continues and moves so fast that you then look back and say, "Where has the time gone?"

Chapter 4

MY SECOND MARRIAGE

(Misused)

After thirty years of marriage, my parents were on the verge of separating. At the time, I was occupying a first-floor apartment in their home with my baby girl. Momma was spending more time at our little storefront church than at home, and Daddy was doing his usual construction jobs away from home. I never thought that they were not getting satisfaction out of their lives. It never crossed my mind that they weren't in love with each other anymore. But Daddy had several jobs outside of his regular job, and Momma was always at the church.

All their children were adults or teenagers, so there was no need for them to be home with us. At different times, many of us lived in the first-floor apartment along with several tenants and relatives. There was always someone living in our house. Even Momma and Daddy lived in the apartment, and we lived on the second and third floors at one time.

One day, some musicians began to visit our church. One of the guys liked my younger sister and became busy trying to impress her. He also brought a friend along with him to introduce to me. He was a flashily dressed guy. He could play an organ in a way that made it sound like a cool, heavenly instrument. He really impressed me with his biblical knowledge and eventually made me realize that my first husband was gone and wasn't returning. His dad was a bishop, and he was brought up in the Church of God in Christ (COGIC). COGIC people were holy roller people. They shouted, sang, and preached and shouted, sang, and preached and shouted, sang, and preached—you get my message?

Eventually, we began to date, got married, and had a child. I was now twenty-five years old. My second husband was an excellent organist and was well sought after by churches. He didn't have a regular job other than playing the organ. I will never know how I fell for him. All he had to offer was that he had plenty of biblical knowledge, was a bishop's son, and played the organ.

He would come over to see me while we were dating. Sometimes, we had Bible study, and other times, he played music with my dad. Since Daddy seemed to like him, I thought, well, he must be the man for me. My mother didn't think much of him. She thought he was a typical musician and a womanizer. That's exactly who he was. How could a man who was raised in church as a bishop's son be so conniving? Well, he was! Eventually, he was practically living in my apartment. My daughter was three years old at the time, and I decided that she needed to go to daycare because Momma was busy with church, and her dad couldn't attend to her during the daytime. I enrolled her in a nearby Christian daycare where my new man's father was the overseer. She was a good little girl, and his father would sometimes take her to his office if I was late picking her up, which made her and myself feel special.

Because his father was a bishop, he didn't approve of our lifestyle and was constantly pushing us to marry. That Christmas, we got married and moved into a townhouse apartment. Meanwhile, my mom and dad separated. It was 1977, five years after my first marriage. I still don't know why I married him. He was the most jealous man I ever met. I was afraid to speak to friends I knew from school or our neighbors because I would have to explain to him who they were to me. We started fighting from the first week of marriage to the very end.

One weekend, he asked me where I was getting ready to go. I guess he didn't like my answer and he hit me so hard that I fell to the floor. When I got up, he was going out the door. He had a CB (citizens band) radio system in the trunk of his car, and I knew he was going to turn on his CB radio. I got in my car with my daughter and strapped her in the front seat. I pulled the car in gear to drive and then raced toward him.

He reached into his trunk, grabbed a wrench, and threw it so hard that it went through the car window and landed on the floor of the driver's side. I reversed my car to hit him or at least jam his legs between the cars. Before I could do that, he jumped in the trunk of his car. I remember hearing a voice say, he's going to kill you, or you're going to kill him.

I reversed my car to drive off, but behind me was a policeman with his siren on. He stopped me and said they had a call that a woman was trying to run over a man. I was so upset. I told him that my husband had hit me so hard that I fell on the floor. I even showed him the wrench that my husband had thrown at my daughter and me. He could have killed us both. The policeman said, "Ma'am, you need to file an assault charge on him, but you can't try to run him over."

I went to do just that, and my husband knew where I was going. He was such a coward and was always afraid of going to jail. When I got back home and went upstairs, he came begging for forgiveness, telling me how sorry he was and that he was leaving to go over to his parents until I cooled off. He said he would check on us the next day.

A few weeks later, I had a doctor's appointment. I had been taking birth control pills, but they had become so effective that my doctor took me off them for a month. One day, my friend at the bank was saying she was on her period, and I said, "You can't be because my period is just before yours." Girlfriends talked about those kinds of things back then.

A few days later, I set up a doctor's appointment to get back on the pill. The doctor told me to bring my first morning urine the day before my appointment. I had my husband drop it off. I was so upset when I found out that the doctor told him to wait for him to test it. I was still naïve; I had no idea he was going to test me for pregnancy before I went back on the pill. I was so disappointed when my husband called me at work to tell me I was pregnant. He seemed overjoyed. I started crying at work, and everyone asked what was wrong. It was one of the worst days of my life!

He and I fought and argued all the time. Finally, I left him during the sixth month of pregnancy and went back to live at my father's house. My eldest sister had moved into the first-floor apartment, so Daddy told me, "You can't stay here. You need to be with your husband."

My sister told him, "She's going to stay down here with me." Within a few weeks, my husband begged me to come home, and because of my father, I went back to him. He stayed out almost every day, but when he was home, I hated him being there. My pregnancy did not stop the abuse. So, we separated again.

Within our three-year period of marriage, we separated five times before I got it together. He messed around with several other women. On one occasion, while getting my daughter from daycare, a little girl came up to me and said that my daughter's daddy was coming over to see her momma. One of the daycare workers grabbed the child and said, "I'll see you tomorrow. Have a good night!"

Anyway, I never wanted any more children, so I asked my doctor to tie my tubes. He told me I had to get my husband to sign papers for me if I truly wanted to get my tubes tied. I had to go find him. When I did, he was with some other woman. I asked him to sign the papers. He said he wasn't going to sign those papers for someone to use me as a good f---!

I said, "I'm going to sit on this car until you sign." He didn't listen; that bastard drove off, and I fell off the car and onto the ground. He had the nerve to call my father and tell him that I tried to pick a fight with him and that he moved the car and I fell off. My dad was so upset, and when he saw him, he told him, "You better leave her alone until she has this baby, or I'll kill you myself." He didn't mess with me after that.

The day I went into labor, my brother and I walked for what seemed like hours. Finally, it was time to go to the hospital. It was 7:30 p.m. when I was taken to the hospital. My mother came and stayed with me. Hours passed, and finally, at 12 a.m., the doctor said, "She's on her way!" Huh, I was sure both of my children were going to be boys.

"How do you know it's a girl?" I said.

"A fast heartbeat means it's usually a girl," he said.

Then, a nurse came in and said, "Your husband is here, but you can only have one person in the room with you." I told her that it was only my brother. He had said he would be here.

"Send my mom in, please," I said, disappointed. I had no idea what I was going to name my baby. Again, I had only picked out a boy's name. Finally, she was born at 12:56 a.m.

Momma was there smiling, saying, "She's so pretty."

I said, "Great, that's good!" I was so tired and sleepy.

Then, she said my baby's daddy was there, and I said, "Let him come in." Well, by the time she kissed me and left, he was already gone!

The next morning, I awoke to him sitting on a chair beside my bed, waiting for me to wake up. Oh, he said he was so sorry and told me how much he loved me and our baby. He had flowers, balloons, and everything. What an ass! He threw me off a moving car with his baby inside me, and now he says that he loves me and our baby? He was there every day, pleading to get back together.

Three days later, my husband was there to take me home. He was at my house every day. He said, "Let's start over and get our own place." I really wanted to get out of my daddy's house for good. We searched and found a nice apartment within a few weeks. We moved in, and he talked me into leaving my job and staying home with our child. I thought it was a good idea, so I went to the office and resigned. For the first three months of being in our new apartment and having our child, he was truly trying to be a good husband and father. Then, he started coming in later and later and fussing, arguing, and finding some issue to fight or complain about. Within six months of that mess, I decided I was done!

One day, while my husband was at work, I packed as much stuff as I could and left. When my daddy saw me that night, he said, "You married that man, and you need to stay with him." Again, my sister told him that I could stay with her. One of my younger siblings was living on the third floor and attending Xavier University, but he didn't mind us being back home. My oldest brother had married and had a son. Three of my siblings and my niece were still in Dayton with Momma. During that time, I went to church regularly.

Within a few weeks, I got a temporary job, which led to permanent employment with a non-profit organization. After working for several months for the non-profit organization, my husband walked into the office and asked for me. The receptionist called to say, "There's someone here to see you." I asked her who it was, and she asked him, "Who's calling, sir?"

When I heard him say, "Her husband," I asked my boss to tell him to leave, and she did just that! She really liked me, and we bonded well. I kept hearing that voice say, he's going to kill you, or you're going to kill him! I couldn't stand the thought of leaving my children alone in this world, and I never looked back. He tried to find out where I lived and who was keeping the kids. I had moved into a Section 8 apartment and got a sitter for my youngest child. My oldest child was in school and participated in after-school care.

During that time, my job title was Accountant/Secretary. I was the HNIC of all the company's financial records. I was in charge of the payroll, paying the company's bills, transcribing the board of trustee's minutes, and I also did whatever the company's director needed assistance with. I worked closely with an attorney who was a title examiner. I asked him if he could recommend a reasonable attorney who would work with me to get a divorce. He spoke with an attorney he knew, explained to him that I couldn't pay much for a divorce, and asked if he would bill me monthly. God rescued me! Within two years, I moved out of that Section 8 apartment into a newly renovated two-family apartment. I had my life back.

My daughters and I lived in the second-floor apartment, and within six months, a tenant moved into the third-floor unit. He was a playboy, eight years my senior, and was a happy-go-lucky kind of man. We became good friends. He always looked after me and my daughters. He would buy food and ask me to cook certain meals for the both of us. His girlfriends didn't like our friendship, and several of them were jealous. They'd let me know that he belonged to them. It was funny to us, and we would laugh about them later.

On numerous occasions, he would ask me to go with him to his motorcycle clubhouse. Sometimes, if I could get my friend to watch my kids, I'd go with him. He was humorous and had a Southern accent. I would have so much fun with him. One summer, my kids were in Dayton with my momma, and we went out almost every weekend. That was how we started dating. I was so mad at him and told him I didn't want to have a relationship with him. I truly loved being his friend. I had totally forgotten about dating anyone.

Once, after divorcing his brother, my ex-brother-in-law told me that I should give up dating, and that was what I had practically done. I had become devoted to my daughters and my career. Somehow, we eventually became lovers and friends. Sometimes, we would go out of town with the motorcycle club to cabarets. Boy, were those cabarets fun! He and I dated off-and-on for about fifteen to twenty years! He asked me to marry him several times, but I always said no. I thought I would lose his friendship and our relationship if we got married. He eventually married someone else, and they got divorced within a few years. It was then that I knew I made the right decision not to marry him; we remained friends until his death.

Chapter 5

SINGLE LIFE

(Restored)

I joined a wonderful church when my children were ten and five years of age. The church had one of the most influential and intelligent pastors I had ever met! He once preached a sermon about King David entitled "The Battles Keep Coming." Well, battles kept coming into our lives, too, and just like with King David, God was always with me.

I continued to work for the non-profit company until the funding ceased. I received a six-month contract to help dispose of the company's assets, train the local government employees to be loan officers, and assist in setting up the program with the City of Cincinnati.

The non-profit staff had to submit resumes for positions with the City of Cincinnati. I assisted those who didn't have resumes in writing theirs. Most of the positions required a college degree (for Black people, anyway). I didn't have a college degree at that time, and boy, did I regret it. I felt substandard and insecure, and it resulted in me being laid off. One of the employees didn't even have a high school diploma, yet he remained employed while I was laid off.

Now, I had two kids and was living in an expensive apartment with no way to pay for it. Funny how I could now understand how my parents felt every time Dad was without work in the winter. I sought unemployment compensation and started reaping the benefits. This allowed me time to spend with my girls and be a stay-at-home mom, just like my mom was when we were growing up. I enjoyed getting the girls ready for school, watching soap operas, cooking homemade meals, and staying up late at night.

Before I realized it, I had only one month of unemployment benefits left, so I had to find a job soon. I started my search, and shortly thereafter, I got a call from the City of Cincinnati for an interview. The interview was with my old boss, who was supervising the same program for which the city had once ceased funding. We were already bonded, and she thought I was an excellent employee—even if I was late all the time. I got hired by the city. At the time, I thought it was the greatest job on this side of heaven, and now that I'm retired, I'm even more grateful for the opportunity.

I had heard that government employees were lazy, over-paid, and worthless. After working there for the first two or three years, I thought the same. The coffee break was from 8:00 to 11:30, lunchtime was from 12:00 to 2:00, and most people left to go in the field from 2:30 to 4:30. Then they got back to the office by 5:00 to sign out. Now, that wasn't everyone, but most of the time, the only people in the office all day were the clerical staff.

For fifteen years, I did both home and business loans; I enjoyed interacting with my clients. While working with homeowners was the most rewarding, I also worked with numerous bankers and became very knowledgeable about businesses, finance, and the corporate world. I packaged and processed loans, trained interns, and presented the loans for approval to a board of lenders, community leaders, and government officials. Everything was time-consuming, and the paperwork was extensive. There were times when the work was stressful, but it was also very educational and rewarding.

Within two years, at the ripe age of twenty-eight, I purchased my first home. My momma was living in Dayton, and I was visiting her regularly, but I very much wanted her to come back to Cincinnati. She was living with almost all my siblings, including one who had a baby girl by this time. The three of us could fit in my house, so Momma finally moved back. The other three siblings were working and remained in Dayton. I was happy for about a year with Momma living with us, but it was getting old, and she knew it. Within fourteen months, my sister and mom got their own apartment and moved out.

Throughout this time, I remained close to a friend I had met while working at the bank. While we had both since left the job, we stayed in touch. We even went to the same church and had become even closer than we ever were. One night, I was feeling down, broken, and disgusted. She felt my pain and showed up at my house unannounced with her boyfriend. "What are you doing here?" I asked.

She said, "I got worried about you. You just didn't sound like yourself, so I needed to come see you." My house felt cold; my friend's boyfriend said the pilot on the furnace had probably blown out, so we went into the basement to see. While we were in the basement, my friend went into my bedroom and put $40 and a note on my pillow. The note said, *God loves you and so do I. He will take care of you.* By the time her boyfriend and I got back upstairs, she was at the basement door asking, "Was everything alright?"

I said, "Everything is fine, except he tried to light the pilot and almost blew himself and the house up."

We all laughed, and she turned to her boyfriend and said, "She's fine now; let's go home." While getting into bed that night, I found her note and the money on my pillow and began to cry and thank God. I called her later and thanked her, and she said, "I knew you wouldn't ask me for anything, but the Lord told me what to do. Please don't try to return my blessing." A few days later, she was telling a guy at work about me, and he sent me $20 and told her to tell me that God loves her and will always provide for us. He was right! I brought groceries, had money for my kids' lunch, and put gas in my car for the entire week. God always makes a way when it seems like there's no way!

Eventually, I had to replace that furnace. I had established several friendships at work, and one of my friends was moving to California. He helped me once when the furnace had completely gone out in my first house. I was so sad when I came to work the next day. It was a cold November. We always talked about what we'd do if we won the lottery. He asked me what was wrong, and I told him about the furnace going out. As soon as I told him about the furnace, he said, "Don't worry, I'm going to hit the lottery and buy you a new furnace."

During lunchtime, he went home and got two electric space heaters, brought them back to work, put them in my car, and told me to put one in my girls' room and one in my bedroom until I was able to get a new furnace. He also gave me some information from a non-profit organization that weatherized homes and had a program that provided furnaces, insulation, and more. The best part of the program was that it was a forgivable loan program if you met certain income guidelines and I qualified. I applied on the phone, met with the contractor for the next few days, and got a new furnace installed within a week! God did it again. I am still close to this friend thirty years later!

That same friend was there for me when my nephew died. A few years later, my daddy also passed. Those were the saddest deaths I had experienced since my first husband's death. My friend volunteered for a non-profit in the evenings to help people with certain kinds of diseases, like my nephew, and he got him help. He was the one who took me to be with my dad at the hospital. He was even there with me at Daddy's funeral and repast. God shows up in all kinds of people. This friend was a white guy who demonstrated to me that God works through all people, no matter what color.

We have stayed in touch, and our love for each other never wavered. We traveled Europe together when I retired and talked on the phone regularly. He was always right here, helping me with all my struggles and concerns. He remembered my birthday even though he refused to let me know his. Every time he came back to Cincinnati, he always made time to see me. One time, he went to Greece alone, but he didn't forget about me. He sent me a beautiful silver necklace and earrings. I almost fainted when I saw the price! His only reason for putting the receipt in the package was in case I had to return or exchange them during their lifetime warranty. God has blessed me with wonderful people despite my sins and disappointments. Thank you, Lord, for your grace and mercy.

Throughout my life, I learned about the prejudices Black people face. It didn't matter how hard you worked or what you had to bring to the table; you wouldn't get any praise no matter how well you did your job. At least, that was how I felt. You were only expected to do what you were told to get an increase.

In 1992, I had established my own credit, but I was in debt and needed home repairs. The administration always used the excuse that I didn't have a degree to not increase my salary. Although I had great performance reviews and got the "maximum raise," my salary was far below that of other city staff. My supervisor knew my capabilities and depended heavily on me, and she advocated for a salary increase. She told them that, regardless of whether I earned a degree or not, I was worth more than most of the employees working there. Personnel (it was called back then) administered a study of the positions in our department. Within six months, I received a $10,000 increase! Hallelujah! God is so good! That amounted to $830 more a month! I paid off debts, and my girls and I began living comfortably!

•

Chapter 6

LIFE GOES ON

(Renewed)

Eventually, my supervisor left and sought employment elsewhere. However, I continued to work for the City of Cincinnati for thirty years, processing both residential and business loans. I climbed the ladder until I could only receive cost of living raises. I spent the last fifteen years as a senior real estate specialist in the law department.

One day, my supervisor said he and another supervisor had taken real estate classes and expressed how much they had learned. He said, "You can take courses if you want, too." I jumped at the opportunity, took those classes, took a real estate exam, and became a realtor. I was asked to become a notary for the loan program, and I became a notary public, too. God knows what we need before we do. I had established another career and another source of income.

By 1991, my oldest daughter was graduating from high school. I needed another stream of income to help pay her college tuition, so I continued working for the city and sold real estate part-time. I loved showing houses and getting ideas from the homeowners. I would sell houses in the evenings and on weekends. Sometimes, I took my daughters with me. I met a lot of people who referred me to other people, and those real estate sales paid my daughter's tuition. I always told my girls that when they turned 18 years of age, they could go to college, and I'd help pay their tuition for four years, or they would get a nice luggage set to move out of my house! I thank God both chose to go to college.

My oldest graduated as the valedictorian, so I didn't have to pay a lot for her first year of college as she received a scholarship. In the latter part of her first year, she got sick and was having terrible stomach pains. As such, her grade point average dropped below 3.0, and she lost her scholarship. She managed to get through the last quarter and came home that summer. She was diagnosed with gallstones and had to have a laparoscopic cholecystectomy (removal of the gallbladder). She recovered within a few weeks and was able to return to college in September. She managed to get her GPA up in the first quarter, and by the second quarter, the school reinstated her scholarship. What a mighty God!

On the other hand, my youngest daughter was struggling in school. After some testing, we discovered she was dyslexic. She spent two years in special education classes. I spent numerous days going back and forth to the school, trying to make sure she would eventually get out of those classes. By the fourth grade, I removed her from the special education classes. Her teacher advised me not to, but the principal thought she'd be fine. By the sixth grade, she was keeping up with all the other students, but by the time she was in the ninth grade, she was skipping math class all the time.

When I got her first report card, I saw that she had an F in math. Needing to find answers, I went to the school and asked the teacher how she could get an F. He told me she only showed up to class once or twice a week. I asked him why he hadn't called me. He said it was his job to teach students, not to make sure they came to class. I was so darn mad at that man that I went to the principal's office and demanded they press truancy charges against her. Of course, the principal said they couldn't do that, but I insisted and eventually convinced him to do so.

The day came when we went to court. My daughter sat in the dark, dreary courtroom chair, acting tough, like she wasn't worried, until the referee said, "Young lady, let me make you understand something. I don't know you, and it doesn't matter to me if I send you down that long hall with shackles on your feet and cuffs around your wrist. There's only one person in this courtroom who cares, and that's the lady sitting next to you; do you understand me? I don't know you."

My daughter looked at me, started crying, and said, "Momma, I'm sorry!" The referee sentenced her to write a hundred-word essay telling describing where she saw herself ten years from now. I never had any more concerns about her skipping class again. I think it was one of the best things I did for her. Today, she's an author and children's book publisher. She's also working in the public school system.

While my oldest daughter was in college, my youngest daughter and I bonded so much that she didn't want to go away to college until her third year. She ended up going to Kentucky State University but came home after a quarter (she eventually got an associate degree from Cincinnati State). After she came home, I put my second home on the market because, one day, my nephew said, "We need a bigger house to have family gatherings." This nephew was like a son to me, and by this time, he had come home from college very sick. He had a terminal illness, and anything I could do to make him happy, I did. I sold our first house and made a $10,000 profit, which I put toward our second house.

Daddy loved our second home and enjoyed it like it was his own house. He had begun to come around to see how the girls and I were doing as soon as I bought my first house, and he kept coming around when we had moved to the second one. I wanted a deck added to the property, so after a quick trip to Home Depot, I got my brother to build it.

One Saturday, I was having Bible study with a group of ladies, and my dad came over. He politely asked me who built that deck. When I told him that my brother did, he said, "Call him over here right now, and you can go back in the house to yo' meeting." By the time we adjourned our Bible study, Daddy and my brother were rebuilding that deck. Daddy asked me, "Couldn't you see that deck wasn't level?"

My brother said, "Why didn't you call him to build it?" He and Daddy were in and out of the basement, repairing a broken window covered by the deck and leveling the deck boards. My brother was mad as hell, but he dared not say anything to Daddy. He just kept working and sweating for a few hours.

Then, my dad said, "Come here and look at your deck now." You could really tell the difference. "Don't you ever do your sister like that again."

"Yes, sir, next time, I'll tell her to call you," my brother said. My daddy went home smiling. He was always there to fix something in my house and showed his love for all of us, even though he never said, "I love you" until the day he died.

We had parties and barbeques on that deck all the time. I loved that house, but it was much too large for me. My girls had gone off to college at that point—one had even met a guy and got married. I sold that home, made a handsome profit, and then purchased a smaller ranch in the beautiful Amberley Village.

Chapter 7

LED BY GOD

In 2001, I grew very close to one of my coworkers; we became best friends. She was very smart and encouraged me to go back to school for my degree in real estate, which led to me becoming a real estate broker. The City of Cincinnati had educational incentives and would reimburse employees for each passing grade, so there was no reason I shouldn't have gotten my degree. I ended up getting an associate degree in real estate and opened my own company. This was one of the best things I accomplished while working for the city.

One day, I was sitting in my office, talking with another coworker, when the phone rang.

"How can I help you?" I asked.

"I'd like to know what happened with my uncle."

"Who is your uncle?"

"John Frost."

I became upset immediately. It was John's nephew who was born after my first husband's death. "Who's your mother?" I asked. When he responded, I asked him, "Why don't you ask your momma?"

He said, "No one in my family will talk about it." I angrily explained how hateful and disrespectful his mother was to all my family after John died. I began crying profusely—so much so, that I had to leave work. It was as if John's death had just happened. Eventually, John's nephew apologized and asked if he could meet with me to talk.

What he didn't say was that he was in school to become a private investigator and that wanted to use John's death as a case study (his mother apparently encouraged him to do so). I agreed to meet him and invited a few of my family members to meet with us. The sad part of this meeting was that I realized I was still hurting thirty years later after John's death. Not only was meeting him healing, but it was also forgiving. For once, I got to tell someone in his family the truth and how I felt about it. I was relieved. This nephew helped me heal thirty years of agony, built-up pain, and guilt that I didn't realize was still inside of me.

Since I started selling properties, most of my deals were from my friends, family, and anyone else they referred me to. At the time, one of my friends I met at work was living in apartments, paying the IRS every year, and buying expensive cars. Once I told her to buy a house, she asked me a few questions and then said, "Let's find me a house." She used me as her agent and has referred numerous clients to me. Another work friend utilized my services to sell her house and purchase another one. My friend from high school continuously sent me clients, and my friend from the bank never ceased to direct people to me, too. I've only used word-of-mouth advertising to sell real estate. God has blessed all my efforts, and like the old folks used to say, "I found out if you make one step, God will make two."

I am now a real estate broker and continue to sell homes through word of mouth and referrals. I've purchased five homes and an office building. I've established many relationships throughout my life, and I thank God for each and every one of them. I've taught biblical classes and joined two major churches. Through it all, I've learned to trust in Jesus and talk to the Lord. I am now seventy years old, and though I suffered from bad relationships, past sins, and errors, I'm thankful to God Almighty for every experience.

After retiring at the ripe age of fifty-seven, I acquired a certification as a notary public signing agent. This allowed me to establish another career in closing loans. God is great! I give all honor and praise to Him! I continue to thank God for every accomplishment, no matter the hardship and struggles it took to receive them. You may think you get through life on your own strengths and efforts, but it's only by God's grace and mercy. I know it's only through God that I'm still here today, and I thank Him for the opportunity to share my life experiences with you.

The adversary loves to stir up your past and interfere with your life when things seem good—that's when you praise God. One day, my eldest daughter and I went to Jungle Jim's. While we were shopping, I got a phone call from an old schoolmate, Penny, telling me about our fiftieth reunion. It was a happy hour gathering at Jaid's Place to celebrate the class of 1972. I said, "I don't give a darn about a class reunion. I don't care about you people ever since John died. All y'all did was spread rumors about me. Do you really think I would come to that?"

She said, "I don't know what you're talking about, and I don't understand why anyone wouldn't come to our reunion." I don't know why, but at the moment, my pain clouded my judgment, and I lashed out at her for no real reason and hung up the phone. But what the devil meant for bad, God meant for good. The next day, I got a text from Penny reminding me to go to the happy hour. Again, I thought I had been healed from John's death, but I guess God knew there was still some unfinished healing that needed to take place, so trusting His judgement, I decided to go that weekend.

As soon as I walked in, several of my old classmates greeted me with love and happiness. I was amazed and so happy I went. Then, Penny came up to hug me and said, "I'm so glad you came out." We all had a great time that night. When the happy hour was over, she and I talked about school and why I was so angry when she called. I knew it was the Lord who made that happen.

The next week, I met up with my classmates again. As I sat with them, we started looking at our 1972 yearbook. Someone started showing me all the people in our class who were now deceased. I don't know if I'll make it to the next class reunion, but I sure hope so, and I'm so glad God has let me get this far.

I've been to many places and met many people who set stumbling blocks in my path, but I have many loved ones whom God has blessed me with. My children may or may not realize the consequences we suffered in getting to this place in life, but God knows. When I look back and see where God has brought me, I continue to say thank you, Lord! Many peoples' stories may never be told, but I thank God for letting me tell my story, and I pray it might help whoever reads this book march forward with God as their guide.

Chapter 8

RELATIONSHIPS

Pastor Harper was a great man. He was my pastor for 24 years. I learned to love Bible study and enjoyed his services at Morning Star Baptist Church. He never made me feel ignorant about the Bible and always answered my questions. I can recall several of his sermons and explanations of scripture. He was always thorough and reassuring about God's word. It was so comforting and soothing, especially to learn about God's promises. Although there were times I felt I could never please God, I was comforted by Pastor Harper's words. I referenced one of his sermons, "The Battles Keep Coming," earlier in the book. He talked about King David's life and the many battles he fought.

One night, several of my classmates in Bible study were saying what a lousy father David was; I couldn't believe it. Though David sinned, he was still a man after God's heart. Another time, we were studying the Book of Job, and it occurred to me that God kept both King David and Job as they went through one catastrophe after another. So why was I concerned, worried, or despondent with the nay-sayers, gossipers, evildoers, and negative people? I had to look to God for all my questions. I had to become interdependent on friends, family, and those whom God put in my life, but mostly, I needed to seek out the kingdom of God. Some people come into our lives for a season, some a lifetime, and some for a moment. Some come to help us, and some people come to be helped.

Proverbs 18:21 says, "Death and life are in the power of the tongue, and those who love it will eat its fruits."[4] Proverbs 15:4 says, "A gentle tongue is a tree of life." Proverbs 31:26 says, "She opens her mouth with wisdom, and the teaching of kindness is on her tongue." Gentle words are a tree of life; a deceitful tongue crushes the spirit. Kind words heal and help; cutting words wound and maim. The tongue that heals is a tree of life, but a devious tongue breaks the spirit.

My spirit was broken and crushed for a long time, but I have just begun to heal. Hurt people do hurt people. According to Billy Hallowell, "Chaos and division have become rampant in culture, with snips, snipes and nasty rhetoric dominating much of our discourse. The dynamic has led many Christians to seek opportunities to find

---

[4] *ESV Study Bible*. 2016. Wheaton, IL: Crossway Books.

faith-affirming and God-centered content and to take steps to improve their own contribution to dysfunction."[5]

We live in a dysfunctional universe and must depend on God to persevere through life. I need you; you need me, and together, we can be what God wants us to be.

In writing this book, I felt like an outcast. I was lonely and hurt, but talking with my friends and daughters made me realize that I could love again; I didn't need to be a people pleaser; I needed to be a God seeker. Relationships make us strong. We can rely on each other as we seek God's guidance. I've been sick, hurt, distraught, and thought I wanted to die, and whenever death seemed too close, I sought God, and He said, not yet I'm not through with you. Although I felt reprehensible about some of my past decisions and didn't want to share them, I'm at peace knowing I have someone who may need to hear my story.

I feel free for the first time in fifty years. I know the battles will continue to come, but more importantly, I know God has never, ever forsaken me and will continue to be with me in every battle. Looking back, I regret allowing malicious gossip, more than any

---

[5] Hallowell, Billy. "Power of Life & Death': Verses about the Tongue & Watching Your Mouth." Great American Pure Flix, March 29, 2023.
https://www.pureflix.com/insider/bible-verses-about-the-tongue.

disaster I have experienced, to influence some of my decisions. If I could say anything to help anyone endure in life, it would be to listen only to God. Tell God about everything, even the tiniest thing you think of. Confide only in the Lord. Yes, children should obey their parents, but parents need to talk to the Lord, too!

No one on this earth is or was perfect but Jesus! Mistakes, mishaps, accidents, errors, and sins happen. Pray, pray, pray, ask for forgiveness, and keep moving forward. We all have sinned and fallen short of God's glory, but don't give up on God because He won't give up on you. I don't know what tomorrow holds for my life now, but I know I can't make it another day without God's guidance. There's no way I would tell you that I don't regret some of my past, but I will tell you God has kept me.

I pray I haven't excluded anyone who helped me along the way, and I pray for your forgiveness. I love each one of you and pray for success in your life with Jesus. The most influential people in my life expressed their love and acceptance of me, both good and bad. They loved me despite my imperfections. I thank God for my pastors, biblical teachers, and spiritual advisors who helped me learn and grow in God's grace. Pastor Harper always said that whenever you're going through things, and it seems it's more than you can bear, ask God what lesson He wants you to learn. I don't know what lesson I could learn from John's suicide or my second husband's mistreatment of me. However, I got through it all, and I learned to trust in Jesus and God because He kept me here for a reason, which may be why He permitted me to tell my story.

I read my Bible every day and learn something new each time. I'm encouraging you not to give up on God because He won't give up on you! I've achieved a good life through all my struggles, and I thank God for His joy! Happiness is based on circumstances, but joy is a direct gift from God! When I began writing this book, I didn't want to mention any names for fear of hurting someone; I thought it was best to let people guess who I was talking about. But I realized I was still stuck on what people would have to say. People pleasers are fantasies that will never happen. I finally realized I can't let people dictate my life. This is my story; this is my song; I'm going to praise my Savior all my days long!

www.ingramcontent.com/pod-product-compliance
Lightning Source LLC
LaVergne TN
LVHW051158080426
835508LV00021B/2680